Thurgood Marshall

Thurgood Marshall was the first African American to serve as an associate justice on the United States Supreme Court.

JUNIOR ■ WORLD ■ BIOGRAPHIES

A JUNIOR *BLACK AMERICANS OF ACHIEVEMENT* BOOK

Thurgood Marshall

G. S. PRENTZAS

CHELSEA JUNIORS

a division of CHELSEA HOUSE PUBLISHERS

Chelsea House Publishers

EDITORIAL DIRECTOR Richard Rennert
EXECUTIVE MANAGING EDITOR Karyn Gullen Browne
EXECUTIVE EDITOR Sean Dolan
COPY CHIEF Robin James
PICTURE EDITOR Adrian G. Allen
ART DIRECTOR Robert Mitchell
MANUFACTURING DIRECTOR Gerald Levine
SYSTEMS MANAGER Lindsey Ottman
PRODUCTION COORDINATOR Marie Claire Cebrián-Ume

JUNIOR WORLD BIOGRAPHIES

SENIOR EDITOR Kathy Kuhtz

Staff for THURGOOD MARSHALL

COPY EDITOR Laura Petermann
EDITORIAL ASSISTANT Mary B. Sisson
SERIES DESIGN Marjorie Zaum
PICTURE RESEARCHER Wendy P. Wills
COVER ILLUSTRATION Daniel Mark Duffy

First Printing

1 3 5 7 9 8 6 4 2

Library of Congress Cataloging-in-Publication Data
Prentzas, G. S.
    Thurgood Marshall / G. S. Prentzas.
    p. cm.—(Junior world biographies)
    Includes bibliographical references and index.
Summary: A biography of Thurgood Marshall.
ISBN 0-7910-1769-9
0-7910-1969-1 (pbk.)
    1. Marshall, Thurgood, 1908–1993. 2. United States. Supreme Court—
Biography. 3. Judges—United States—Biography. I. Title. II. Series.
KF8745.M34P73 1994
347.73'2634—dc20
[B]
[347.3073534]
[B]
                                                            92-34222
                                                                 CIP
                                                                  AC

Contents

Civil rights lawyer Thurgood Marshall reviews his notes before arguing the most important case of his career, Brown v. Board of Education of Topeka, in which he asserted that segregation was unconstitutional.

1

"That Is Not What Our Constitution Stands For"

On the morning of December 8, 1953, lawyer Thurgood Marshall walked up the marble steps of the U.S. Supreme Court Building in Washington, D.C. He looked up at the four words chiseled across the front of the large white marble building: Equal Justice Under Law. Marshall wanted to make those words ring true.

This was the day that Marshall would give his closing arguments in the most important case in his career as a *civil rights* lawyer. Civil rights are the personal and property rights of every citizen, recognized by a government and guaranteed by a constitution and its laws. The case, known as *Brown v. Board of Education of Topeka*, was a combination of five different lawsuits. African-American students and their parents—including Topeka, Kansas, parent Oliver L. Brown—had sued their local school boards in Kansas, Delaware, South Carolina, Virginia, and the District of Columbia. They claimed that *segregation*—the policy of keeping people of different races separate—in public schools violated the U.S. Constitution. The U.S. Constitution is the document that outlines the basic laws and principles under which all citizens of the United States are governed.

In each of the five lawsuits, the parents and students had lost. They all filed an *appeal*, asking the nation's highest court, the *U.S. Supreme Court*, to review the lower courts' decisions. By agreeing to hear the *Brown* case, the Supreme

Court now had to answer a question important to millions of Americans: Are segregated schools unconstitutional?

The *National Association for the Advancement of Colored People (NAACP)* provided the lawyers for the parents and students in the *Brown* case. Founded in 1909, the NAACP had fought for decades against racial *discrimination* and segregation. Discrimination is the unfair treatment of an individual, group, or race. The *integration*, or the act of opening to people of all races without restriction, of the nation's public schools had been one of the NAACP's main goals since the 1930s.

Thurgood Marshall had joined the NAACP as a lawyer in 1934. Now, 19 years later, the 45-year-old attorney hoped for a major legal victory in the *Brown* case. If he won, the Supreme Court would rule that the nation's segregated school systems were unconstitutional. But if Marshall lost, most African-American children would continue to receive an inferior education in poorly equipped schools.

Marshall planned to win the *Brown* case by convincing the Supreme Court to overturn the *separate-but-equal doctrine*, which it had established in an earlier case, *Plessy v. Ferguson*. In that 1896 case, an African American, Homer Adolph Plessy, had been found guilty of breaking a Louisiana law that required black passengers to ride in train cars separate from whites. Plessy appealed his conviction to the Supreme Court. His lawyer argued that government-enforced segregation of blacks and whites violated the U.S. Constitution's *Fourteenth Amendment*, which guarantees all citizens "the equal protection of the law."

The Fourteenth Amendment had been adopted in 1868, five years after President Abraham Lincoln's Emancipation Proclamation freed enslaved African Americans in the South. The Fourteenth Amendment was meant to guarantee newly freed blacks the same legal rights as whites. But in its *Plessy* decision, the Supreme Court upheld the Louisiana segregation law. The Court ruled that the races could legally be separated, as long as the facilities provided for blacks and whites were equal.

The *Plessy* decision encouraged some states, counties, and cities to pass laws that required racial separation in housing and public facilities. These laws were also called Jim Crow laws, a term that originated in a character from minstrel shows during the late 19th century and that became another expression for racial discrimination. By 1900, African Americans in many states were restricted to "blacks only" drinking fountains, railroad cars, movie theater sections, hospitals, and schools. As long as these facilities were judged to be equal to those reserved for whites, racial separation was legal under the separate-but-equal doctrine. The judgments about what was "equal," of course, were usually made by whites who only wanted to keep the races separated. Segregation soon became the law of the land.

Faced with the task of defeating this long-standing tradition of segregation, Marshall entered the courtroom. Spectators, both black and white, filled every seat. Many had waited outside in the biting cold since before dawn. The nine justices of the Supreme Court soon took their seats, and the court session began.

Marshall's rival, 80-year-old John W. Davis, rose from his seat to speak first. The distinguished constitutional lawyer had begun his closing remarks on the previous day. He now summed up his side's position, arguing that the separate-

In the early 1950s, young students attend a one-room school in the South. Prior to the 1954 U.S. Supreme Court decision on the Brown *case, many of the country's African Americans had to enroll in racially separate, inferior schools.*

but-equal doctrine had become a basic part of American life. Claiming that equality had been achieved, Davis asked the Supreme Court to uphold segregation in public schools.

Marshall then rose to make his final statement. "I got the feeling on hearing the discussion yesterday that when you put a white child in a school with a whole lot of colored children, the child would fall apart or something," he said. "Everybody knows that is not true. These same kids in Virginia and South Carolina . . . play in the streets together, they play on their farms together, they go down the road together, they separate to go to school, they come out of school and play ball together."

Marshall insisted that the only way for the Supreme Court to approve school segregation laws would be to find that for some reason blacks were inferior to other human beings. He ended his remarks by saying, "The only thing [segregation] can be is an inherent [inborn] determination that the people who were formerly in slavery, regardless of anything else, shall be kept as near that stage as is possible. And now is the time, we submit, that this Court should make it clear that that is not what our Constitution stands for."

As with all their cases, the justices discussed the *Brown* case in secret session. On May 17, 1954, the Supreme Court announced its decision. Chief Justice Earl Warren read the Court's opinion. He began by discussing the separate-but-equal doctrine and the Fourteenth Amendment. Chief Justice Warren then reviewed earlier segregation cases and outlined the history of education in the United States.

An hour after he had begun reading, the chief justice still had not announced the Supreme Court's ruling. Finally, at 1:20 P.M., he reached the important question: "Does segregation of children in public schools solely on the basis of race . . . deprive the children of the minority group of equal educational opportunities?"

Chief Justice Warren paused for a moment. Then he said, "We believe that it does." He went on: "To separate [African-American children] from others . . . solely because of their race generates a feeling of inferiority . . . that may affect their hearts and minds in a way unlikely ever to be undone."

Nearing the end of the opinion, the chief justice read, "We conclude . . ." then he hesitated, raised his eyes from the document, and added, "unanimously." A shock wave seemed to sweep the courtroom. Chief Justice Warren continued, ". . . that in the field of public education the doctrine of 'separate but equal' has no place. Separate educational facilities are inherently [by nature] unequal." By a nine to zero vote, the Supreme Court had ruled that school segregation was, indeed, unconstitutional.

News bulletins interrupted radio and TV programs, announcing the Supreme Court's ruling in the *Brown* case. Thurgood Marshall and a colleague heard the news of the decision at the NAACP's New York office. Years of struggle had finally paid off in victory.

A snapshot from Marshall's family album shows him at two years old. His aunt, Media Dodson, once remarked that Thurgood was a beautiful baby with big, dark eyes.

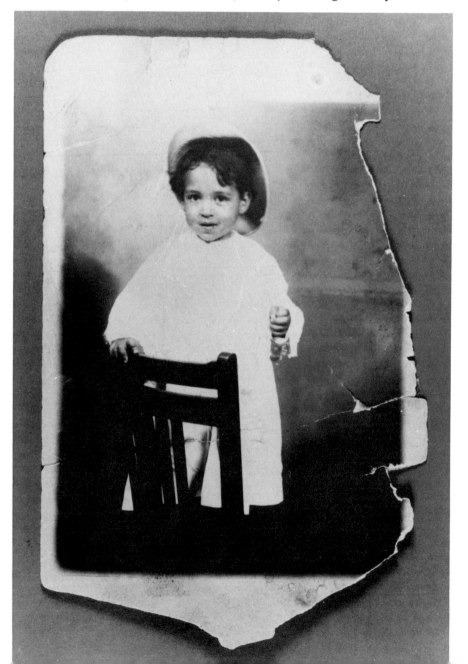

2

First in His Class

Thurgood Marshall was born on July 2, 1908, in West Baltimore, Maryland. His father, William Marshall, worked as a dining-car waiter for the Baltimore & Ohio Railroad. The job was a good one, especially for an African American at the beginning of the 20th century. Norma Marshall, Thurgood's mother, taught in a segregated Baltimore elementary school. The Marshalls resided on Druid Hill Avenue in West Baltimore, a middle-class neighborhood where black and white families lived together peacefully.

Thurgood was named after his grandfather, Thoroughgood Marshall, a former slave. ("By the time I was in second grade," Marshall later told an interviewer, "I got tired of spelling all that and shortened it.") According to his aunt, Media Dodson, Thurgood was a beautiful baby with big, dark eyes. She remembered him as a "timid" little boy. But, Dodson told a *Time* magazine reporter, "one day—he must have been around five—he stopped crying and became a pretty tough guy."

Thurgood's mother, Norma Arica Marshall, was a teacher at an elementary school in Baltimore, Maryland. A talented pianist and singer, Norma Marshall was a strong person and a leader; she had a great influence on her son.

Thurgood remained "a pretty tough guy." His unruly behavior got him into trouble many times. His grade school principal often sent Thurgood to the school basement when he misbehaved. Thurgood could not return to class until he had memorized a passage from the U.S. Constitution. "Before I left that school," Marshall later told a reporter, "I knew the whole thing by heart."

Parts of the Constitution, however, baffled Thurgood. He wondered about the Fourteenth Amendment's guarantee of equal rights. He saw inequality all around him, including in his own segregated school. Thurgood asked his father what the Fourteenth Amendment meant. William Marshall replied that the Constitution described things as they should be, not as they really were.

Years later, Marshall said that his father had guided him toward a career in law. William Marshall followed court cases as a hobby and sometimes took Thurgood to the courthouse to watch trials. "He never told me to become a lawyer," said Marshall, "but he turned me into one. . . . He did it by teaching me to argue by challenging my logic on every point, by making me prove every statement I made."

A bright student, Thurgood could have coasted through school, getting good grades with little effort. But Norma Marshall urged her son to work hard and to use his mind. As a high school student, Thurgood led a busy life. He earned top grades, joined school clubs, tried out for several sports, and attended dances. After school, he delivered supplies for a hat company.

The Marshalls gave their son a stable and loving home. But they could not protect him from racial *prejudice*. Prejudice is a feeling or opinion, usually negative, that has been formed about something or someone before all the facts are known. One afternoon, Thurgood was carrying a tall stack of hatboxes. He arranged the boxes as best he could in order to board a trolley. As he carefully stepped up to the streetcar, he was sud-

William Marshall, Thurgood's father, guided his son toward a career in law. The elder Marshall often followed court cases as a hobby and sometimes took Thurgood to the court-house to watch trials.

denly grabbed by the arm and yanked backwards. "Nigguh, don't you push in front of no white lady again," snarled a male voice.

William Marshall had told his son never to tolerate racist remarks. Thurgood and the white man argued and began to fight. A white policeman separated the two men and took them to the police station. For a black man, hitting a white man was dangerous in the early 20th century, especially in a southern state, such as Maryland. Marshall could have gotten a beating, a jail sentence, or worse. The policeman, however, did not arrest either man and soon released both of them. Marshall had been brave. He had also been very lucky.

Thurgood graduated from high school in 1925. Like his older brother, Aubrey, who was a medical student, Thurgood wanted to continue his education. But in the 1920s, African-American students who wanted to go to college had few choices. In the South, state laws did not allow white colleges to admit blacks. White colleges in other parts of the country accepted only a few black students each year.

Marshall decided to apply to Lincoln University in Oxford, Pennsylvania, the nation's oldest African-American college. At that time, about half of Lincoln's graduates went on to study medicine, dentistry, education, or law.

Like many other college students, Marshall played more than he studied during his first few years. Despite his fun-loving nature, Marshall had a B average in his courses. He read many books dealing with the African-American experience in the United States. Marshall especially liked the writings of the eminent scholar, editor, and activist W. E. B. Du Bois and the works of poets Countee Cullen, Jean Toomer, and Langston Hughes.

While attending church with friends one Sunday, Marshall met Vivian Burey, a senior at the University of Pennsylvania. They fell in love al-

Marshall (middle row, second from right) sits for a class portrait as a Lincoln University freshman in 1925. While at Lincoln University, Marshall, like many of his classmates, enjoyed playing more than studying; however, he maintained a B average in his courses.

most immediately and were married on September 4, 1929. The young couple moved into a small apartment in nearby Oxford. To help pay for his education, Thurgood earned money as a bellhop and waiter. Vivian, who had graduated from college by this time, worked as a secretary. She had a calming effect on her high-spirited husband. A friend later commented, "She helped 'turn him around.'"

Marshall received an A.B. (bachelor of arts) degree, with honors in the humanities (literature, philosophy, and the arts) in June 1930. A talented public speaker, he decided that he wanted to become a lawyer. He applied to the respected law school of the University of Maryland. But the all-white university, which had never admitted a black student, turned him down.

Marshall then applied to Howard University's law school, which accepted him. The university, located in Washington, D.C., was founded in 1867 as a school for newly freed slaves. Then, as now, many of the nation's African-American doc-

At Howard University, Charles Hamilton Houston, a very intelligent lawyer and a pioneer in the civil rights movement, taught Marshall how to use existing laws to combat racial injustice.

tors, lawyers, dentists, and engineers held degrees from Howard.

Recalling his first week in law school, Marshall said that he knew "this was it. This was what I wanted to do for as long as I lived." Marshall worked hard in his courses, and it paid off. At the end of his first year, he was named top student in his class.

Marshall greatly admired two of his law professors, William Henry Hastie and Charles

Hamilton Houston. Hastie, a Harvard graduate, later became the nation's first African-American federal judge. Houston was a brilliant attorney and a pioneer in the civil rights movement. Both men taught their students how to use existing laws to fight against racial injustice.

Judge William Henry Hastie speaks with members of a youth group in Louisville, Kentucky, during the 1940s. When Marshall was a second-year law student at Howard, Hastie asked Marshall to prepare a brief for a North Carolina desegregation case.

Under the supervision of Hastie and Houston, Marshall and his classmates joined late-night sessions at which lawyers planned their strategies for civil rights cases. In 1932, Hastie asked Marshall, then a second-year law student, to prepare a *brief* (a written argument presented to a court by a lawyer) for a North Carolina *desegregation* case. (Desegregation is the ending of racial separation.) Although his side lost the case, Marshall learned a lot about the actual practice of law.

In 1933, Marshall graduated first in his class. Harvard University offered him a scholarship—a grant of money—to continue his studies, but he turned it down. Marshall wanted to do what he had worked so hard to do—practice law. He took the bar examination, a test required by each state before it allows a lawyer to practice, in Maryland. Passing the test with flying colors, Thurgood Marshall was ready to battle in court on behalf of his clients.

In 1933, Marshall set up his own law office in Baltimore, Maryland. Although he had no clients the first year, he soon became known as "the little man's lawyer" who represented poor people needing legal assistance.

3

The Little
Man's Lawyer

Thurgood Marshall began his law career by set-
ting up a small office in Baltimore. In 1933, when
Marshall started his practice, African-American
lawyers were rare. But despite their small num-
bers, they had trouble attracting clients. Because
almost all judges and jurors at that time were
white, African Americans usually hired white
lawyers to represent them, believing that a black
attorney could not win their case.

During his first year as a lawyer, Marshall
had no clients. He had to pay $1,000 for office

expenses, a lot of money in those days. But eventually, people who needed legal assistance began to show up at Marshall's door. Tenants who were evicted from their homes for not paying rent and victims of cruel and harsh treatment by the police came to Marshall for legal help. Although most of them could not afford to pay him, the young attorney turned no one away. He soon became known as "the little man's lawyer." Representing poor clients did not make Marshall a rich man, but working on their cases helped make him an outstanding lawyer.

Word of Marshall's courtroom skills soon spread. He started to attract paying clients. In 1934, Marshall was chosen to be the lawyer for the Baltimore chapter of the NAACP. Like most of Marshall's jobs, the position paid nothing. But Marshall felt honored to work for the civil rights group.

Marshall's first NAACP case involved a protest against stores on Baltimore's Pennsylvania Avenue. Although their businesses depended on

African-American customers, the white store owners refused to hire black employees. The NAACP had urged people to *boycott* the stores, that is, not to shop there, until the owners promised to employ African Americans. When sales at the stores fell, the shopkeepers sued the NAACP to stop the protest. Marshall and Charles Houston, his law school professor, defended the NAACP. Working as a team, Marshall researched the case, and Houston presented it in court. The judge, shocking almost everyone in the courtroom, ruled in favor of the NAACP. He even complimented Marshall and Houston for their impressive legal presentation.

Marshall soon joined the NAACP's nationwide effort to bring an end to segregation. In the 1930s, African Americans faced discrimination and injustice in many areas of life, including education, employment, and housing. The NAACP decided to start its campaign for racial justice with legal attacks on segregated graduate schools in the South. Victory in a small number of these cases, NAACP officials hoped, would lead to integration at all levels of education.

The NAACP chose to attack segregated law schools first. They hoped that judges, who were lawyers themselves, would easily understand that "separate" law schools could never be "equal." Teaming up again with Charles Houston, Marshall won his first major case in 1935. His client, Donald Murray, a 20-year-old college graduate, had been denied admission to the University of Maryland's law school. University officials told Murray that he could obtain "separate but equal" education at Maryland's Princess Anne Academy, a segregated institution.

Explaining that the academy did not offer a law degree, Murray again applied for admission to the University of Maryland. He was told that the university did not accept students of his race. Murray then took the university to court. Marshall and Houston argued his case, which came to trial in June 1935. Houston persuaded Raymond A. Pearson, the president of the university, to admit that the separate facilities at Princess Anne Academy were unequal.

After hearing all of the evidence, the Baltimore City Court ordered Pearson to admit Murray to the university's law school immediately. Marshall appeared calm and serious as he listened to the verdict. But when he left the courtroom with his wife and parents, he showed his true feelings by taking Vivian into his arms and dancing a lively tango.

In 1936, Charles Houston, then serving as special counsel to the NAACP, asked Marshall to become his assistant. For the next two years, Marshall and Houston worked closely together. They

Marshall (standing) and Charles Houston (far right) work on their legal strategy for Donald Gaines Murray's (center) suit against the University of Maryland in 1935. They won their case and Murray became the first African American admitted to the university's law school.

traveled from one southern courthouse to another, filing lawsuits for African-American students and teachers. When he was not on the road with Houston, Marshall divided his time between New York City—headquarters of the NAACP—and Baltimore. He kept a small office in his family's home to serve his many poor clients.

In 1936, Marshall handled his first case as NAACP assistant special counsel. This lawsuit involved Lloyd Gaines, an African-American college graduate who had applied to the law school at the University of Missouri. Rejecting Gaines because of his race, the university offered to pay his tuition at an out-of-state law school.

Represented by Houston and Marshall, Gaines sued the state of Missouri. In November 1938, after Missouri courts had ruled against

One of the officials for the NAACP points to the group's latest recruitment poster in its New York City headquarters.

Gaines, the Supreme Court agreed to hear the case. Rather than challenge the separate-but-equal doctrine, Marshall and Houston demanded equality as outlined in the Fourteenth Amendment. If Missouri refused to let Gaines attend its all-white law school, it must offer him—and other qualified black applicants—an equal law school.

By a vote of six to two, the Supreme Court agreed with Marshall and Houston. State laws that called for segregation, ruled the Court, were legal only if they provided the separated races with equal facilities within the state. Because Missouri did not have an equal law school for African Americans—and could not afford to build one— the state had to let Gaines enroll at the University of Missouri.

In late 1938, Charles Houston resigned as NAACP special counsel because of poor health. Marshall, now 30 years old, replaced him. He and Vivian moved into a walk-up apartment in Harlem, a large African-American community in New York City. As the NAACP's top lawyer, Marshall was now the nation's most prominent African-American attorney.

In October 1939, Marshall was appointed director-counsel of the NAACP Legal Defense and Education Fund. The fund provided free legal aid to African Americans who suffered injustice because of their race. As director of the fund, Marshall was in charge of all legal activities for the NAACP. He planned its overall courtroom strategy, oversaw individual lawsuits, wrote briefs, and often argued cases himself. During its early years, the fund aimed at two major targets: laws that prevented African Americans from voting and laws that required segregation in transportation and other public facilities.

In 1944, Marshall won a Supreme Court case that made racial discrimination in primary elections—where voters choose their political party's candidates for office—illegal. Two years later, Marshall won an important segregation case involving Irene Morgan. The African-American woman had boarded a bus in Virginia bound for

Maryland. Ordered to sit at the back of the bus as required by Virginia law, she refused. The driver called the police, who arrested Morgan and fined her $10. Marshall took Morgan's case all the way to the Supreme Court. The Court ruled that segregation on buses traveling between states was illegal. This decision eventually led to the end of segregated transportation in the United States.

That same year, 1946, Marshall was awarded the NAACP's highest award, the Spingarn Medal. Named for longtime NAACP chief Joel Spingarn, the medal is presented each year for the "highest or noblest achievement" by an African American. A struggling Baltimore lawyer only 13 years earlier, Marshall had beaten the odds facing any aspiring African American in the 1930s. He had become one of the nation's best-known attorneys and one of its most powerful crusaders for social justice.

In 1945, North Carolinians quench their thirst at separate drinking fountains.

Marshall (center) escorts Autherine Lucy (front row, left) to the district court in Birmingham, Alabama, in February 1956. Marshall later obtained an order forcing the University of Alabama to admit Lucy as a student.

4

The Fight Continues

In the late 1940s, Thurgood Marshall and his NAACP colleagues began to fight for better housing for African Americans. At the time, integrated neighborhoods were rare in the United States. Most African Americans lived in ghettos in the cities or in the run-down sections in smaller towns. Even if a black family could afford a home in a white neighborhood, few white owners would sell or rent them any property.

In many white neighborhoods, home buyers signed written agreements promising that they would never sell or rent their houses to anyone of a different race. In many cities and towns, whole neighborhoods signed these agreements, making all the homes in the area unavailable to African Americans.

In a case known as *Shelley v. Kraemer*, Marshall asked the Supreme Court to outlaw these agreements. "This case," he told the Court, "is not a matter of enforcing an isolated private agreement. It is a test as to whether we will have a united nation or a nation divided into areas and ghettos solely on racial . . . lines."

In May 1948, the Supreme Court ruled that the nation's courts could no longer enforce such agreements. Marshall had scored another victory. Blacks and other minorities would continue to face many difficulties in trying to move into white neighborhoods. But now they had the full weight of the Supreme Court behind them.

By this time, Thurgood Marshall had earned a nickname from newspeople: "Mr. Civil Rights." Marshall had won many battles against segregation, but he knew that there was yet a long way to go to reach the goal of racial justice. African Americans still found few educational opportunities open to them. For example, in the southern states there were 40 medical schools for whites but only 1 for blacks.

Marshall and the NAACP continued their attack on segregation in education. In one lawsuit, the University of Texas in 1946 had refused to admit Heman Marion Sweatt to its law school because of his race. Sweatt sued, and a Texas judge ruled that the state must either open an "equal" law school for African Americans or admit Sweatt to the law school at the University of Texas.

Texas responded by renting two rooms for a campus and hiring two African-American law-

Homes in an Atlanta black neighborhood contrast sharply with the Georgia State Capitol in this photograph, taken in the late 1940s.

yers as faculty. Sweatt sued again, this time with Thurgood Marshall as his lawyer. Marshall argued that Sweatt could not get an equal education at the law school, which the state had quickly put together. But the Texas Court of Appeals ruled that the state had provided equal opportunities for Sweatt. Marshall appealed the case to the Supreme Court. Meanwhile, in another case, Marshall represented George McLaurin, a 68-year-old African-American college professor. McLaurin had decided to seek a doctorate in education, but the University of Oklahoma refused to admit him because of his race. Marshall convinced an Oklahoma court to order the state to admit McLaurin to the school.

University officials let McLaurin enroll. But they made him sit outside classroom doors during lectures, gave him a screened-off desk in the library, and allowed him to eat in the school cafeteria only when no white students were dining. University officials said that their treatment of McLaurin was legal under Oklahoma's separate-

(Top) Young southerners, all dressed up for their class portrait, pose for this picture outside their meager schoolhouse. Most of the South's black schools were understaffed and overcrowded compared with its white schools (bottom).

but-equal laws. A federal district court agreed, and Marshall appealed the decision to the Supreme Court.

The Supreme Court heard the Sweatt and McLaurin cases on the same day in April 1950. Marshall hoped that the Court would strike down the separate-but-equal doctrine. Instead, the Court ruled that Texas had not offered Sweatt equal educational opportunity and ordered the University of Texas to admit him. The Court also ordered the University of Oklahoma to treat McLaurin the same as all students. But in neither case did the Supreme Court say that the separate-but-equal doctrine was wrong. Marshall had won the battle but not the war. "Separate but equal" remained the law of the land.

Marshall's next big case was a South Carolina lawsuit brought by Harry Briggs and 19 other African-American parents against the Clarendon County school board. The parents wanted the county to provide their children with schools equal to those it equipped for white children. Thurgood

Marshall and his associates, however, hoped that this would be the case in which they could finally defeat the separate-but-equal doctrine.

Clarendon County's African-American community had sought improvements in its schools for years. Local white school officials claimed that black students were being treated fairly. But there were huge differences between the county's schools. For the county's 276 white children, there were 2 brick schoolhouses, 1 teacher for each 28 children, flush toilets, cafeterias, and school buses. The county's 3 black schools, serving 808 pupils, offered a sharp contrast—rickety wooden buildings, 1 teacher for each 47 children, outhouses, no lunchrooms and no school buses.

If Marshall won this case, proving that the county's black schools could never be equal to its white schools unless they were integrated, he could change the nature of civil rights in the United States. If he lost, or if the court only made the school board improve the black schools, he would merely have strengthened the separate-but-equal doctrine.

Attorney Robert Figg, representing the Clarendon County School Board, admitted that the county's black schools were inferior and promised to improve them. Marshall quickly told the court that he wanted to show that the state's segregation laws were unconstitutional. He presented witnesses who described the poor condition of the county's black schools. Experts testified about the psychological consequences of segregation on African-American children. Despite Marshall's efforts, the court ruled in favor of the county. Marshall quickly appealed the decision to the Supreme Court.

The Court agreed to hear the case along with four other NAACP desegregation suits from Delaware, Kansas, Virginia, and the District of Columbia. Titled *Brown v. Board of Education of Topeka*, the combined appeals went before the Supreme Court on December 9, 1952. For three days, both sides presented their arguments to the justices. On his way out of the courtroom, Marshall's opponent, attorney John W. Davis, said to a colleague, "I think we've got it won."

The following June, the Supreme Court announced that it wanted both Marshall and Davis to explain their arguments in more detail. Their next Court appearance was scheduled for December 7, 1953. With the help of 85 prominent scholars, Marshall wrote a new brief. In the brief, he discussed the purpose of the Fourteenth Amendment. "There can be no doubt," wrote Marshall, "that the framers were seeking to secure and to protect [the African American] as a full and equal citizen." Earlier Supreme Court decisions, he continued, made it clear that "school segregation . . . is at war with the Amendment's intent."

Davis told the Court that Marshall's argument was nothing more than an effort to prove that African-American children would be happier or would become better students in integrated schools. And, he added, Marshall had not even proved *that*. The justices of the Supreme Court disagreed with Davis. Five months later, they declared school segregation unconstitutional by a nine-to-zero vote.

Marshall later described his reaction to the decision: "I was so happy I was numb." His joy, however, was soon replaced by sorrow. Vivian Marshall told her husband that she was dying of cancer. Although she had known about her illness for months, Vivian had kept it to herself. She did not want to take her husband away from his work on the *Brown* case.

During the following winter and fall, Marshall spent every available minute with his wife. He stayed by her bedside constantly for the last six weeks of her life. Vivian died in February 1955. "I thought the end of the world had come," Thurgood said later.

On September 8, 1954, two Virginia schoolgirls attend a racially mixed class for the first time in their lives at a Fort Myer elementary school.

Most Americans believed the end of segregated schools had come with the *Brown* decision. But segregation would not go away so
easily. Five weeks after the Supreme Court made
its ruling, the governor of Virginia said, "I shall
use every legal means at my command to continue
segregated schools in Virginia." Similar responses
echoed throughout the South.

The *Brown* decision declared school segregation unconstitutional, but it did not say when
integration had to take place. After a hearing in
May 1955, the Supreme Court required public
schools to desegregate "with all deliberate speed."
The states could take whatever time they needed
to integrate their schools, as long as they showed
"good faith." In spite of Marshall's plea for a
specific date for the completion of desegregation,
states gained time to delay. Justice for African-
American children, which had seemed within
reach a year before, once again became a long-
term goal.

On September 12, 1958, Marshall and his wife, Cissy, walk down the steps of the U.S. Supreme Court Building after the Court decided to order the Little Rock School Board in Arkansas to proceed with integration at Central High School.

5

Public Service

Although the *Brown* decision gave Thurgood Marshall the feeling of deep personal satisfaction, Vivian's death and his busy work schedule placed a lot of stress on the 47-year-old attorney. A new development in his private life, however, helped ease the strain. In late 1955, Marshall began courting Hawaiian-born Cecilia Suyat, an NAACP secretary known to her friends as Cissy. In December 1955, they married.

A few months later, Marshall attended a meeting of civil rights lawyers in Atlanta, Georgia. After hearing how slowly schools were being integrated, he urged the attorneys to keep up the pressure. During the next few years, Marshall and other civil rights lawyers filed hundreds of lawsuits demanding integration. These highly publicized cases were met with anger and defiance throughout the South.

The most violent resistance to school desegregation took place in Little Rock, Arkansas. In the fall of 1957, Arkansas governor Orval Faubus sent Arkansas National Guard troops to Little Rock's Central High School. He ordered the soldiers to keep nine black students, who had registered at the all-white school, from entering the building. Governor Faubus ignored several court orders—including one obtained by Marshall—directing that he not interfere with the integration process. For the next three weeks, the students were met each morning by armed soldiers. The teenagers also had to walk through a mob of whites screaming racial slurs and threatening to hurt them. President Dwight D. Eisenhower had to send U.S. Army troops to Little Rock to enable the students to enter the school.

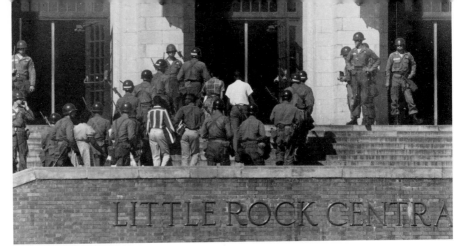

President Dwight D. Eisenhower sent U.S. troops to Little Rock to provide African-American students with protection as they enter Central High School. Despite the 1954 Supreme Court ruling on the Brown *case, Governor Faubus refused to permit integration in the state's public schools.*

In addition to fighting for integrated schools, Marshall and the Legal Defense Fund attacked other areas of segregation. He and his colleagues won African Americans the right to use state-supported beaches in Maryland, to live in city-owned housing in Missouri, to play on public golf courses in Georgia, to eat in railroad station restaurants in Virginia, and to sit in the front of buses in South Carolina.

As the nation entered the 1960s, many concerned Americans began to take part in nonviolent protests against racial discrimination. For example, blacks sat at "whites only" restaurant counters and occupied train and bus seats traditionally reserved for whites. Peaceful civil rights demonstrators were arrested throughout the South. In 1960, Marshall promised "the whole force of the NAACP" to defend these protesters.

In 1961, Marshall worked on—and won—his last case as NAACP chief counsel. Although still firmly committed to the organization that he had served for 27 years, Marshall was offered a new challenge. In September 1961, President John F. Kennedy nominated Marshall for a judgeship on the Court of Appeals for the Second Circuit, which serves the states of New York, Vermont, and Connecticut. In the federal court system, a *court of appeals* hears appeals of decisions handed down by federal district courts. The rulings of appeals courts are final unless they are overturned by the U.S. Supreme Court.

Civil rights supporters greeted Marshall's nomination with cheers. But there was no joy among southern white conservatives, who did not want to see a liberal black lawyer on the federal bench. Nominees for federal judgeships must be approved by the *Senate Judiciary Committee*. The committee, then headed by Mississippi senator James O. Eastland, dragged out Marshall's confirmation hearings for months. Although the civil rights champion was harassed by some senators, he made it through the hearings without losing his temper. The committee finally approved Marshall's nomination by a narrow margin. The full Senate then quickly confirmed Marshall by a 54–16 vote. All 16 votes against Marshall were cast by southern Democrats.

Marshall took his seat on the federal bench in September 1962. During his three years as a circuit court judge, not one of his 98 majority opinions was ever overturned by the Supreme Court. This remarkable record did not go unnoticed in the White House.

One day in July 1965, Marshall and some co-workers were eating lunch when an aide arrived with a message. "The president is on the phone," said the aide.

"The president of what?" asked Marshall.

"Of the United States, sir," replied the aide.

Marshall picked up the phone and spoke to Lyndon B. Johnson. The president invited Marshall to come to Washington, D.C., to talk about a new job.

When Thurgood Marshall arrived at the White House, Johnson asked him to accept the nomination to the post of *U.S. solicitor general*, the person who represents the U.S. government in all cases that appear before the Supreme Court (except those in which the attorney general of the United States chooses to appear). Although it meant a cut in pay and giving up a lifetime appointment as a federal judge, Marshall accepted the president's offer.

Marshall's confirmation hearings were scheduled for July 29, only two weeks after the nomination was announced. The Senate Judiciary subcommittee approved Marshall's nomination as solicitor general in exactly 29 minutes. The following day, the full Senate confirmed him with no debate. Thirteen days later, Marshall was sworn in by Supreme Court associate justice Hugo Black.

As solicitor general, Marshall also decided which cases the Justice Department would ask the Supreme Court to review, which cases lost before lower courts should be appealed, and what position the government should take on cases being heard by the Supreme Court. His duties as solicitor

On August 24, 1965, Marshall is sworn in as U.S. solicitor general while his family and President Lyndon B. Johnson look on.

The Marshalls pose with their sons, Thurgood, Jr. (left), and John William, in the 1960s. Although he was very busy with court cases, Marshall found time on weekends to play touch football with his sons.

general kept him very busy. Nevertheless, he found time to enjoy his homelife. His family by now included not only his wife, Cissy, but two sons, Thurgood, Jr., and John William. The boys, who attended Georgetown Day School, played touch football with their father on weekends. Cissy Marshall's many activities included planning the family's frequent dinner parties, which were attended by some of the nation's most influential people.

During his spare time, Marshall enjoyed listening to jazz and symphonic music and watching movie westerns. Sometimes, he would watch TV reruns of his old favorites for hours. As he once explained, he was "still waiting to see one showing where the Indians win." Marshall also liked to cook, a skill that he had learned as a boy from his grandmother. He often prepared meals for friends, who praised his she-crab soup (a Baltimore specialty), his pig's feet, and his many horseradish-laden recipes.

At the office, Marshall worked hard. He won 14 of the 19 cases that he argued for the U.S. government between 1965 and 1967. He was comfortably settled in both public and private life. But the president of the United States had greater plans for his solicitor general.

In 1967, Cissy Marshall helps her husband put on his robe before he is sworn in as an associate justice of the U.S. Supreme Court.

6

Justice
Thurgood
Marshall

On the sunny morning of June 13, 1967, President Lyndon Johnson and Solicitor General Thurgood Marshall faced a row of television cameras in the White House Rose Garden. The president had just nominated Marshall to fill a vacancy on the U.S. Supreme Court. Marshall had himself argued 32 cases before the Supreme Court and had won 29 of them. "He is the best qualified by training and by very valuable service to the country," declared President Johnson. "I believe it is the right thing to do, the right time to do it, the right man, and the right place," he added, "I believe he has already earned his place in history, but I think it will be greatly enhanced by his service on the Court."

Millions of people celebrated Marshall's nomination. Floyd B. McKissick, chairman of the Congress of Racial Equality (CORE), a leading civil rights organization, said, "This has stirred pride in the breast of every black American." In a letter to the president, Supreme Court Chief Justice Earl Warren wrote, "All of us know Thurgood, and will welcome him to the Court in the belief that he will make a real contribution."

Some people, however, were not thrilled by Marshall's appointment. Marshall's confirmation hearings turned out to be even more heated than those he had endured for the position of circuit court judge in 1961. Southern senators, such as Strom Thurmond of South Carolina and Sam

Ervin of North Carolina, did their best to humiliate the nominee during the hearings. Marshall calmly responded to their hostile questioning, and the full Senate approved Marshall's appointment by a vote of 69 to 11.

One month later, on October 2, 1967, Marshall took the oath of office. Seated next to President Johnson, the proud Marshall family—Cissy, Thurgood, Jr., and John William—looked on as Thurgood swore to "administer justice without respect to persons, and do equal right to the poor and to the rich."

A frank, direct questioner in court and a skillful debater at the justices' conferences, Marshall quickly gained a reputation for plain speaking. Behind the scenes, Marshall's relaxed, straightforward nature set him apart from the formal manner of most judges. Sometimes, however, fellow justices found his informal style unsettling.

Warren Burger, who became chief justice after Earl Warren's retirement in 1969, apparently

On October 23, 1967, the justices of the U.S. Supreme Court pose for a formal portrait. The high court's newest member, Thurgood Marshall, stands at the far right. Associate Justice Marshall became known as "the Great Dissenter" because he found he often had to dissent, or disagree, with the majority of the Court, who were reluctant to rectify racial injustice.

needed a little time to get used to Marshall. In *The Brethren*, their 1979 book about the Supreme Court, authors Bob Woodward and Scott Armstrong quote Marshall's usual greeting to Burger in the halls of the Supreme Court Building: "What's shakin', Chiefy baby?" At first, Burger would simply look perplexed, mumble a few words in response, and walk on. But as time passed, Burger grew to respect Marshall and the two men established a friendly relationship.

Marshall's easygoing personality, however, was misleading. Beneath his casual appearance, he was as sharp and tough-minded as ever. In the decades that followed his appointment to the high court, he firmly defended constitutional rights and equality for all races.

In the beginning of his service as an associate justice, Marshall usually found himself voting with the Supreme Court's liberal majority. Liberal justices tended to be more broad-minded and tolerant of the ideas of others, favoring the freedom of individuals to act or express themselves in a manner of their own choosing. With the election of President Richard M. Nixon in 1968, however, the Court became more *conservative*. Conservatives prefer the existing order and tradition, viewing proposals for change with suspicion. The Republican president replaced retiring justices with members of his own conservative beliefs. Marshall soon became an outspoken *dissenter* (a judge who disagrees with the opinion of the majority of the Court). As an associate justice, Marshall never hesitated to make his feelings known. Outside the courtroom, however, he made few public statements.

Although Supreme Court justices almost never talk about political issues, Marshall did speak out in a 1987 interview. He could not resist answering a reporter who asked him to comment on President Ronald Reagan's contributions to the African-American community. "Reagan," snarled the justice, "has done zero for civil rights."

In September 1989, after 22 years on the Supreme Court, Marshall made a few more political remarks, this time before an audience of federal judges. Supreme Court decisions of recent years, he said, had shown an increasingly narrow approach to civil liberties. And such decisions, he maintained, "put at risk not only the civil rights of minorities but the civil rights of all citizens." The Court, he declared, was now reversing 35 years of progress on civil rights. "We could sweep it under the rug and hide it," Marshall said angrily, "but I'm not going to do it."

On June 27, 1991, Thurgood Marshall announced his retirement from the Supreme Court. When the 83-year-old justice was asked by a reporter what was wrong with him, he replied, "What's wrong with me? I'm old. I'm getting old and coming apart." Looking back on his 24 years on the high court, Marshall said, "I did what I could with what I had." Asked what he was going to do with his time now, Marshall candidly remarked, "Sit on my butt."

In August 1992, retired Supreme Court Justice Thurgood Marshall became the first recipient of the American Bar Association's civil rights award, which bears his name. The association established the Thurgood Marshall Award to recognize and encourage people who have made significant contributions to the advancement of civil rights, civil liberties, and human rights in the United States.

On January 20, 1993, Marshall was scheduled to administer the oath of office to Vice-President elect Al Gore, a close friend of his. Marshall's deteriorating health, however, prevented him from attending the inauguration. Four days later, on January 24, Thurgood Marshall died from heart failure at Maryland's Bethesda Naval Hospital.

History will record Marshall as the first African-American to serve on the Supreme Court. But his leadership role in *Brown v. Board of Education of Topeka*, the 1954 case that demolished the legal basis for segregation in the United States, was perhaps an even more important achievement.

Marshall holds his granddaughter, Cecilia, on his lap during the 1980s. In 1991, after 24 years of vital service on the U.S. Supreme Court, Thurgood Marshall announced his retirement.

When Marshall began his law career in the 1930s, segregation was a fact of life in the United States. African-American children attended separate schools, bathed at separate beaches, drank from separate water fountains, entered theaters from separate doors. When they grew up, they could only get low-paying jobs. In many parts of the nation, they were denied the right to vote, the right to a fair trial, the right to live where they wanted to live.

In convincing the U.S. Supreme Court to rule school segregation unconstitutional, Marshall scored a colossal victory. The decision by no means ended school segregation or wiped out racial prejudice. In many areas of American life, progress was slow and often painful. But the *Brown* decision changed the prevailing opinion of the nation, paving the way for laws that prohibited discrimination in housing, employment, public facilities, and the military. The decision marked the place in history when the government of the

United States finally stopped supporting racial inequality.

Marshall, as one of the most successful constitutional lawyers of the 20th century, had also served as a symbol of hope and courage to citizens of all races. A New Haven, Connecticut, taxi driver once said of Marshall, "he was like Joe Louis [the great boxing champion] for us. He was the black man who was always there to inspire you. The white folk would send up their best against him, and he would knock them out time after time." Historians agree that, in the long run, no government can succeed without offering justice to all of its citizens. By working to advance African Americans, Thurgood Marshall not only helped improve the lives of all Americans but helped fortify the foundation of American justice itself.

Further Reading

Other Biographies of Thurgood Marshall

Greene, Carol. *Thurgood Marshall: First African-American Supreme Court Justice*. Chicago: Children's Press, 1991.

Haskins, James. *Thurgood Marshall: A Life for Justice*. New York: H. H. Holt, 1992.

Hess, Debra. *Thurgood Marshall: The Fight for Equal Justice*. Englewood Cliffs, NJ: Silver Burdett Press, 1992.

Young, Margaret B. *The Picture Life of Thurgood Marshall*. New York: Franklin Watts, 1971.

Chronology

1908 Born Thoroughgood Marshall on July 2 in Baltimore, Maryland

1929 Marries Vivian Burey

1930 Graduates with honors from Lincoln University

1933 Receives law degree from Howard University; opens law office in Baltimore

1934 Begins to work for the Baltimore branch of the National Association for the Advancement of Colored People (NAACP)

1936 Becomes assistant special counsel for the NAACP

1940 Appointed director-counsel for the NAACP Legal Defense and Education Fund

1946 Receives Spingarn Medal from the NAACP

1954 Wins *Brown v. Board of Education of Topeka*, a landmark case that destroys the legal basis for segregation in the United States

1955 Following death of first wife, marries Cecilia Suyat

1961 Nominated to Second Circuit Court of Appeals by President John F. Kennedy

1965 Appointed U.S. solicitor general by President Lyndon B. Johnson

1967 Becomes first African American to serve on the U.S. Supreme Court

1991 Announces retirement from the Supreme Court on June 27

1992 Becomes the first recipient of the American Bar Association's Thurgood Marshall Award for Outstanding Work in the Field of Civil Rights

1993 Thurgood Marshall dies of heart failure on January 24

Glossary

appeal   a request to have a court's decision reviewed by a higher court

boycott   an act of protest in which a group of people stop buying from or dealing with a store or company in order to obtain certain demands

brief   a written statement in which an attorney provides a court with the main points of his or her client's case

Brown v. Board of Education of Topeka   the 1954 case in which the Supreme Court unanimously ruled that segregation in public schools was unconstitutional; this landmark ruling destroyed the legal basis for segregation in the United States

civil rights   the personal and property rights of every citizen, recognized by a government and guaranteed by a constitution and its laws

conservative   having political or social views that favor the way things are and distrusting changes or reforms

court of appeals   a court that reviews cases on appeal from federal district courts; the United States is divided into 12 circuits (geographical regions), each of which has a court of appeals

desegregation   the ending of racial separation

discrimination   the unfair treatment of an individual, a group, or a race

dissenter   on the Supreme Court, a justice who disagrees with the opinion of the majority of the Court

Fourteenth Amendment   an addition to the U.S. Constitution, which declares that all citizens are entitled to "equal protection of the law"; the amendment was ratified in 1868 to provide citizenship for former slaves and to give them full civil rights

integration   the act or process of ending separation of the races; desegregation

National Association for the Advancement of Colored People (NAACP)   a civil rights organization, founded in 1909, that works to end discrimination against African Americans and other minorities

prejudice   a feeling or opinion, usually negative, that has been formed about something or someone before all the facts are known

segregation the custom or legal policy of keeping people of different races separate from one another

Senate Judiciary Committee a small group of senators responsible for interviewing and approving nominees for federal judgeships; if a nominee is recommended by the committee, the entire Senate then votes to decide whether or not the nominee should be confirmed as a judge

separate-but-equal doctrine the rule, adopted by the Supreme Court in 1896, that made racial segregation legal as long as the facilities for blacks were equal to those provided for whites; for more than 50 years, many states used the rule to segregate the races in public schools, in transportation, and in housing

U.S. solicitor general the Justice Department official who represents the United States government before the Supreme Court and decides what positions the government should take on cases being heard by the Court

U.S. Supreme Court the highest court in the United States; decisions made by the Supreme Court hold for the entire nation and can only be overturned by the Supreme Court itself or by an amendment of the U.S. Constitution

Index

G. S. Prentzas is an editor and writer living in New York City. He holds an A.B. with honors in English and a J.D. with honors from the University of North Carolina.

Picture Credits